Originally published as *Preghiera semplice*
© 2012 by EDIZIONI SAN PAOLO s.r.l.—Cinisello Balsamo (Milano)
English translation by Bret Thoman

Copyright © 2013 by Paulist Press, Inc.

Library of Congress Cataloging-in-Publication Number: 2013942102

ISBN 978-0-8091-6767-8 (hardcover)
ISBN 978-1-58768-325-1 (e-book)

Published in English by Paulist Press
997 Macarthur Boulevard
Mahwah, New Jersey 07430

www.paulistpress.com

Printed and bound in the
United States of America
by Versa Press, East Peoria, IL
August 2013

THE PRAYER OF ST. FRANCIS

Francis of Assisi

ILLUSTRATED BY Giuliano Ferri

Paulist Press
New York / Mahwah, NJ

THE PRAYER OF SAINT FRANCIS

Francis was born in Assisi, Italy, in 1181. He was the son of Peter Bernardone, a wealthy cloth merchant. In the language of his time, his Italian name (Francesco) meant "person from France," although the name originally meant "free."

Francis grew up intelligent and cheerful. At the local church-run school, he learned grammar, French, and Latin. But he especially loved hearing tales of the heroic adventures of loyal and generous knights.

When he was twenty years old, he fought in a battle against Perugia, but was taken prisoner. After he returned to Assisi, his spirit was restless. He felt a great emptiness inside, and he was often silent.

However, in reality, a change was happening inside him, and his life would soon move in a new direction. He began giving money to poor people, he embraced lepers, and one day—while he was praying in the little church of San Damiano—he saw the crucifix move its lips and say to him, "Francis, rebuild my house because it is falling into ruin."

He then understood that the Lord was calling him. And he left everything, including the clothes he was wearing. He did so in order to give himself to the Lord in prayer and to serve the poor.

He later heard a priest read these words from the Gospel, "The disciples of Christ should not possess gold or silver, or take a sack or bag or staff for the journey, or have sandals or an extra tunic, but they should only preach the kingdom of God and penance." Francis then decided to live as a poor man among poor people, without possessing anything, just like Jesus.

By living that way, he attracted the attention of other young people who also desired to follow him and imitate his way of life. Among them was Clare, a pretty girl with blonde hair, who chose to be poor and chaste just like Francis.

Francis died on October 3, 1226, next to a little church called the Portiuncula near Assisi. Outstretched on the bare ground, he praised the Lord one last time, to whom he would soon be united through "Sister Death." It is said that at the moment of his death, a flock of larks rose up in flight from the roof of the hut where he was praying.

The Prayer of St. Francis is traditionally attributed to St. Francis, even though it was actually written long after he died. But the spirit of the prayer is fitting to the Saint of Assisi: love for the Lord, love of neighbor, forgiveness, understanding, peace, and joy all reflect how Francis lived and took inspiration from the Gospel. This made him the most well-known and most beloved saint of all.

Elio Sala

Lord, make me an instrument of your Peace:
where there is hatred, let me sow Love

Where there is injury, let me bring Pardon

Where there is doubt, let me bring Faith

Where there is error, let me bring Truth

Where there is sadness, let me bring Joy

Where there is darkness, let me bring Light.

O Lord, grant that I may not so much seek to be consoled,
as to console

to be understood, as to understand

to be loved, as to love.

For it is in giving that we receive.

It is in denying ourselves that we find ourselves.

It is in pardoning that we are pardoned.

It is in dying that we are born to Eternal Life.

GIULIANO FERRI

Giuliano Ferri was born in Pesaro, Italy, on February 20, 1965. He graduated from the Art Institute of Urbino, specializing in cartoon drawing. He later attended an illustration school directed by Stepan Zavrel.

He has been illustrating children's books for a number of years. He has won numerous awards and has published works in Italy, the United States, China, Japan, England, Germany, Austria, and Switzerland.

He works together with elementary schools and libraries where he conducts workshops on the design and implementation of children's book illustration and the dramatization of the stories taken from his books.

He divides his time between illustrating and community service. In fact, he works in a local community where he uses drama in his work with handicapped children.

Giuliano lives in Pesaro with his wife, Monica, and his three children: Alice, Miriam, and Luca.